Joplin *for* Students

7 Graded Arrangements for Early Intermediate Pianists

Arranged by

Carol Matz

Scott Joplin (1868–1917), a renowned African-American composer and pianist, is often referred to as the "King of Ragtime." He studied classical music as a boy, and had a remarkable ability to improvise at the piano. As a teenager, Joplin worked as a traveling musician before attending college in Sedalia, Missouri. During this time, he began composing and had his first pieces published, including "Maple Leaf Rag." Joplin went on to become the greatest and most influential of all ragtime composers, with 44 ragtime pieces, two operas, and a ragtime ballet.

Joplin for Students, Book 2, is arranged at the early-intermediate level. Key signatures are limited to no more than two sharps or flats, and the pieces appear in approximate order of difficulty. Joplin's original scores often used the tempo marking "Not fast;" therefore, students should avoid playing these pieces too fast (a common performance error with ragtime). One of the biggest challenges for students playing ragtime is the execution of continual left-hand leaps. These pieces have been arranged to reduce left-hand movement, while still retaining the flavor and feel of ragtime.

Alfred Music Publishing Co., Inc.
P.O. Box 10003
Van Nuys, CA 91410-0003
alfred.com

ISBN-10: 0-7390-7104-1
ISBN-13: 978-0-7390-7104-5

Cover portrait by Sarah Vaughan

THE EASY WINNERS

(A Ragtime Two Step)

Scott Joplin
Arranged by Carol Matz

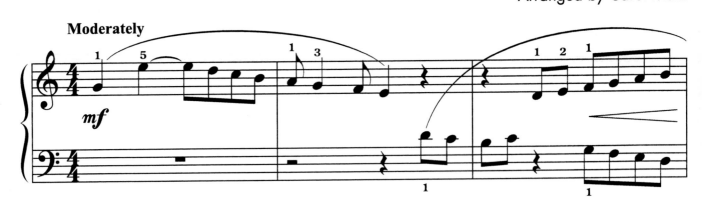

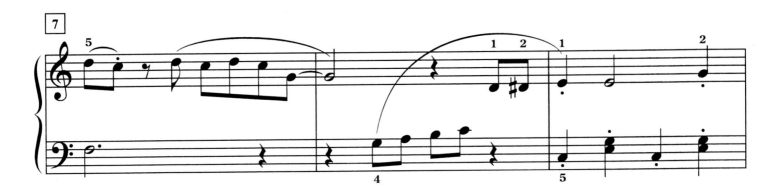

MAPLE LEAF RAG

Scott Joplin
Arranged by Carol Matz

Moderately

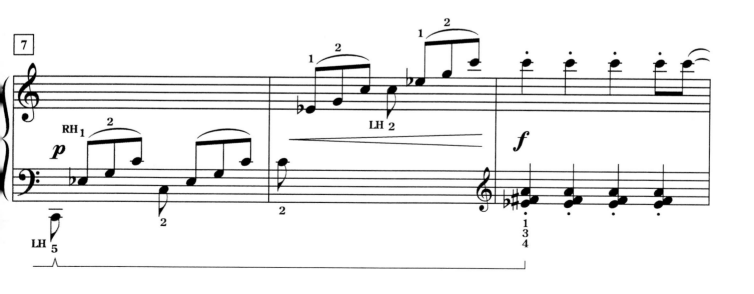

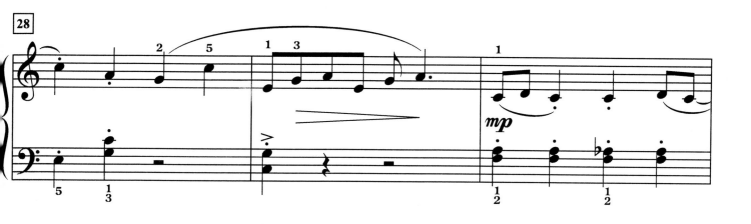

D.C. al Fine

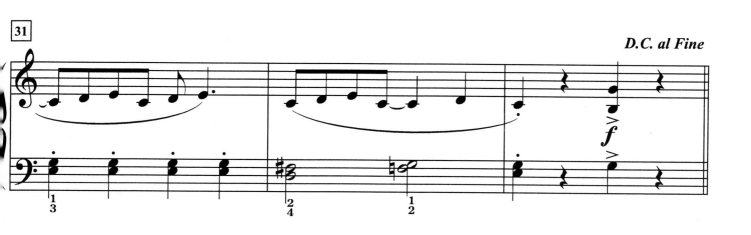

ORIGINAL RAGS

Scott Joplin
Arranged by Carol Matz

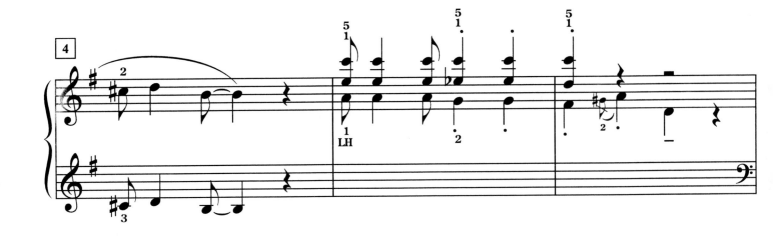

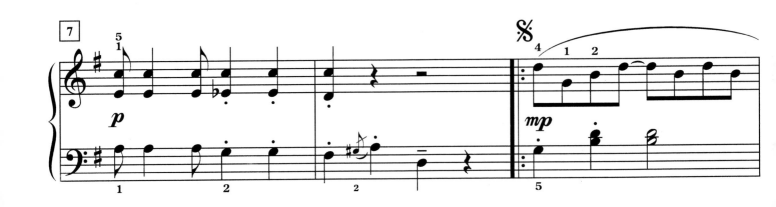

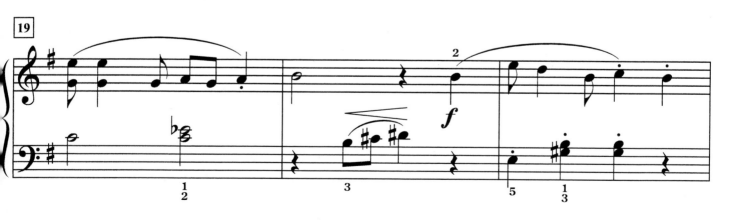

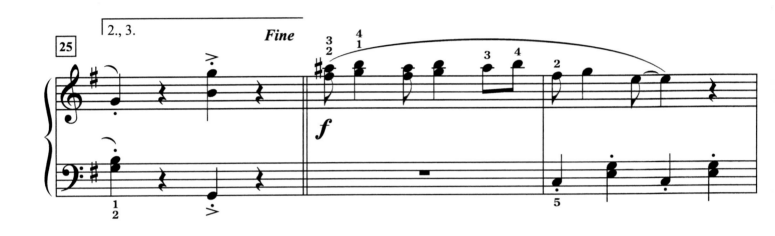

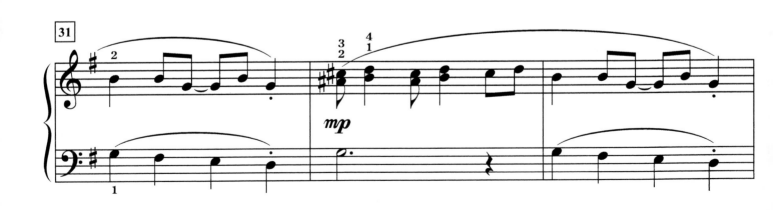

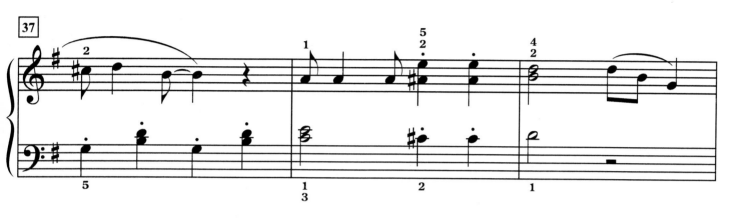

D.S. al Fine

THE ENTERTAINER

(A Ragtime Two Step)

Scott Joplin
Arranged by Carol Matz

* The pedal is optional.

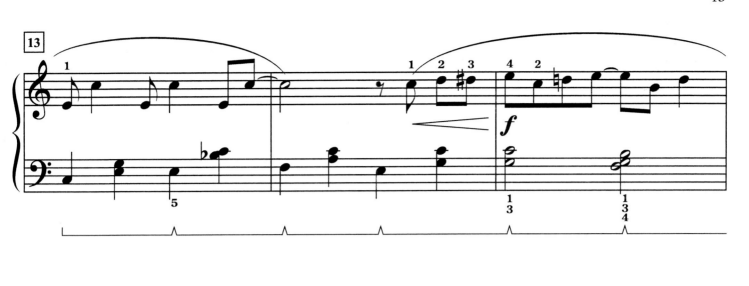

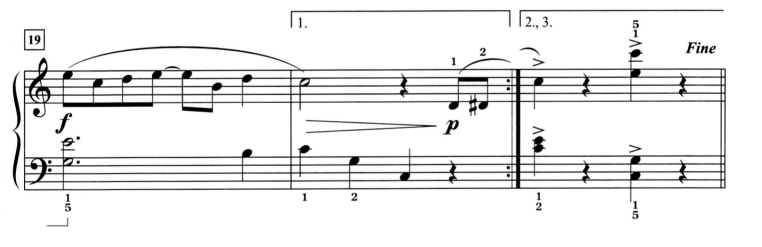

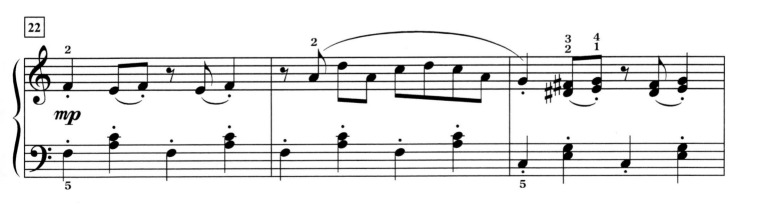

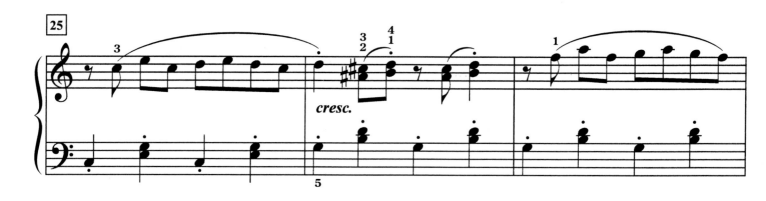

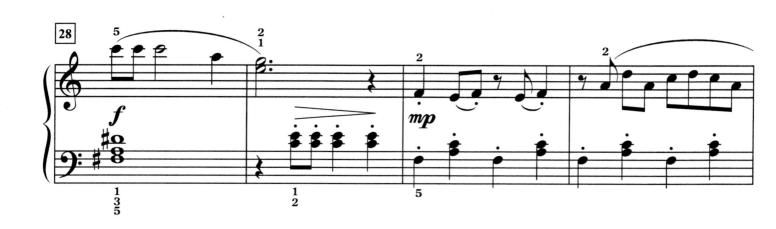

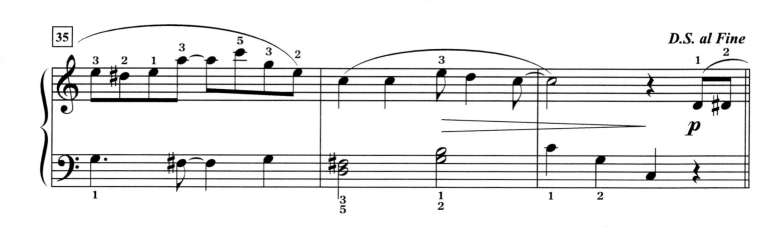

BETHENA

(A Concert Waltz)

Scott Joplin
Arranged by Carol Matz

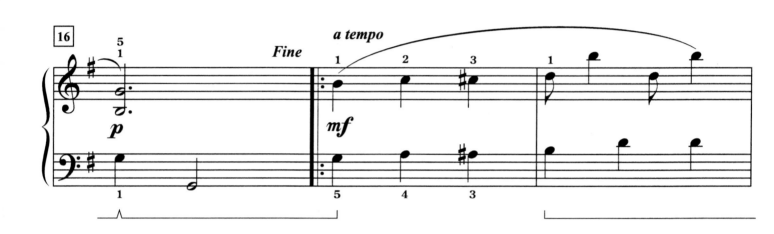

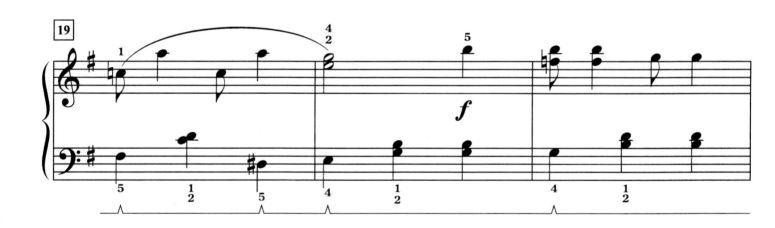

PEACHERINE RAG

Scott Joplin
Arranged by Carol Matz

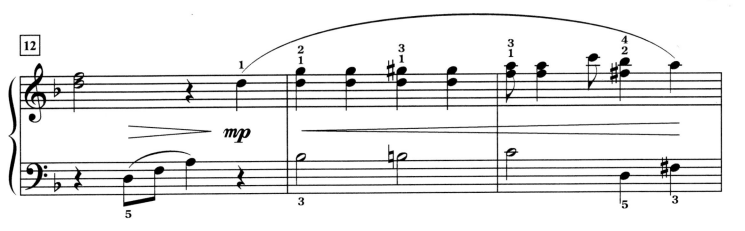

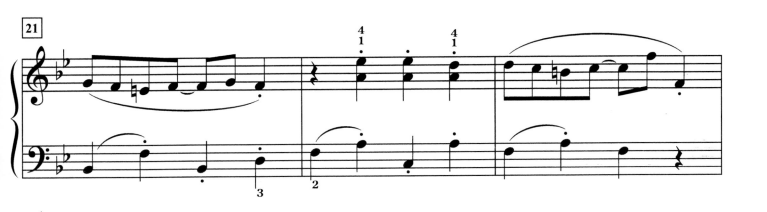

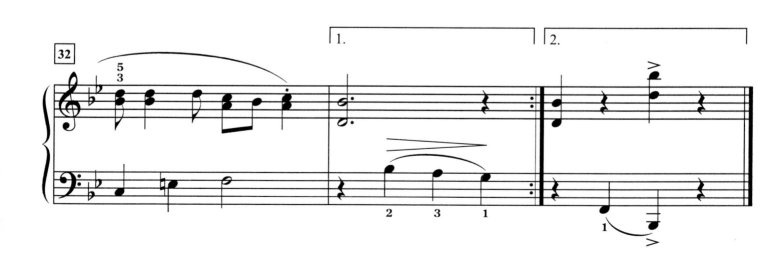

THE CHRYSANTHEMUM

(An Afro-American Intermezzo)

Scott Joplin
Arranged by Carol Matz

Slow march tempo

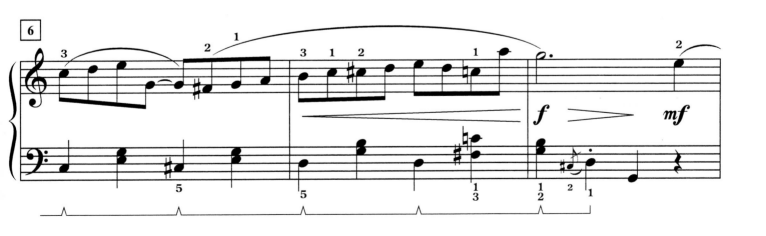